Love, Grief and everything in between

A Collection of 50 Poems

Deepika Pathar

Made with ❤ on the BookLeaf Publishing Platform

www.bookleafpub.in

www.bookleafpub.com

This book is dedicated to:

My younger self

I hope I make you proud.

My husband

My constant support and safe harbour.

My Mother

I hope you're watching over me with pride

My Father

For doing all that you did, to bring me to this day.

Acknowledgement

Many people have contributed to my journey and experiences. But without the ones I list below, I couldn't have found an outlet to turn my joyful and sorrowful moments into writing. Each of you has inspired me and taught me lessons in meaningful ways at different phases of my life.

My husband, Joel Pinto
Thank you for being my person, my safe haven. For nurturing my inner child and walking alongside me on my spiritual journey. For teaching me that self-evolution is the truest form of self-love. For reminding me every day that life is meant to be lived, not reduced to checkboxes. You give me hope, love, and, on most days, life itself.

My babies - Alphie, Chinku, and Coco
Thank you for choosing me to be your mother. You teach me love. You teach me the value of 'now.' You give me so much more

than I ever imagined. You pace me through life. I am, and will forever be, grateful.

Mumma (Mrs. Shobha Pathar) and Papa (Mr. Dilawer Pathar)
I know the value of hard work because you. Thank you for bringing me into this world and contributing in the best ways you could to make me who I am today. I am deeply grateful for your efforts and the sacrifices you made along the way. I understand it wasn't easy.

Vijaya Prakash (Ma'am)
My English teacher, who was more of a friend than a teacher.. I wish you were here today to see how much joy I find in English and reading. I know you're smiling at me from above.

Rumi -The Turkish Poet
Sometimes I wonder if I walked among your disciples when you graced this Earth, because oh, so deeply I am drawn to you. I am forever inspired by your writing— how you embrace

spirituality and pour it so beautifully into words. If I turn out to be even 5% of what you were in your life, I will be grateful. Thank you for showing me the way.

The Girls from Madhav Niwas
Thank you for being my core in my 20s. The world was harsh, and I couldn't have grown without you. You shaped me, and I know on some days, you raised me.

Manisha Pritmani
Thank you for our deep conversations that pushed me to explore my truth. For being my raw and true sister— a refuge I didn't know I needed or deserved until I met you.

Genevieve Williams
Thank you for being my constant and for teaching me the power of choices and courage. I have had the pleasure of knowing many strong women, but to me, you are the strongest. I am proud to have found a friend in you.

Wilma Correa

Thank you for inspiring me every day and showing me, through your example, how to embrace depth, resilience, and kindness. You navigate life with such grace, teaching me the power of compassion in the simplest moments.

Vishal Cherian

Thank you for being the Otis to my Eric. You give me perspective and comfort like very few can. No matter the chaos, life feels so much better knowing you're there.

Ronnie A.K.A Partha

Thank you for being a steady influence in my 20s and even now, for teaching me reflection and correction time and again. While others chased money, you encouraged me to follow my heart, and for that, I'll always be grateful.

Preface

Each poem in this collection is born from personal experience or intimate first-hand observation.

The themes span a spectrum of emotions—from the beauty of love as the ultimate connection, to grief as love's final act, and the countless feelings in between that have deepened my spiritual self.

These poems are not meant to be rushed.
I encourage you to read them one at a time, allowing space to fully absorb each piece.
Each poem evokes its own unique emotion, weaving together a journey through my experience.

The Door

A story pours from every door,
Some make my heart happy, some leave it
sore;
Especially the one where you stood to wave—
I wait there now— would you come again?

I trace your face with my fingertip,
Drawing what lingers of you within my grip.
I see you now, but it strikes me hard:
I can't hear your 'good-bye,' and that breaks
my heart.

I look for you in fragments and figments,
Hoping the universe will drop me a hint,
One that will soothe my grief with a gentle
bind,
And briefly fill the void that you left behind.

For now, I bid you a sweet good-bye,
And in hope, I will let my heart lie,
Knowing that I will return once more,
To meet you before this special door.

Love and Hate

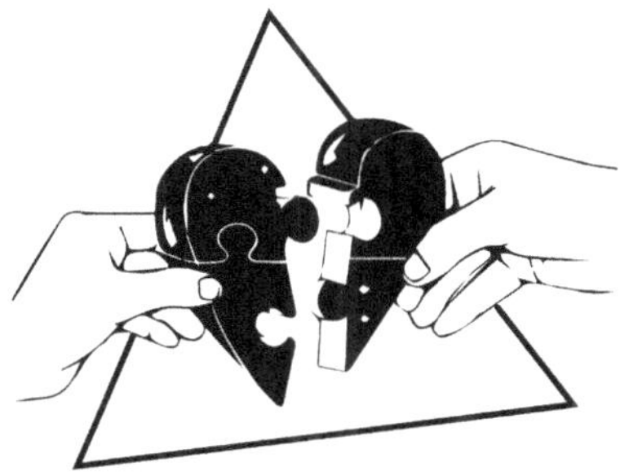

Putting a repeated damper on love
Is pet hate, you can't get rid of,
Do I feel angst for you? I do.
But more often, I feel sorrow for you.

It stands to reason: God is your key,
Mine too, but mine is free,
Stirring me to unclothe of loathe,
To water down my faith entirely, in love.

Does yours lead you otherwise?
Oh, then we must own vastly different skies,
Because I illuminate in a way you don't,
And, unfortunately, you refuge a heart of
stone.

I pray for you to find it in your core,
To feel the spine of humanity to your very
nerve,
To love each one like your own,
To make every corner of the world your
home.

To never cleave mankind again into religions,
To carry messages of love like the good ol'
pigeons,
To rise above your bygone faith,
And free yourself from the weight of hate.

I pray for you to find it in your heart,
To let go and let love play its part.

A Part of You

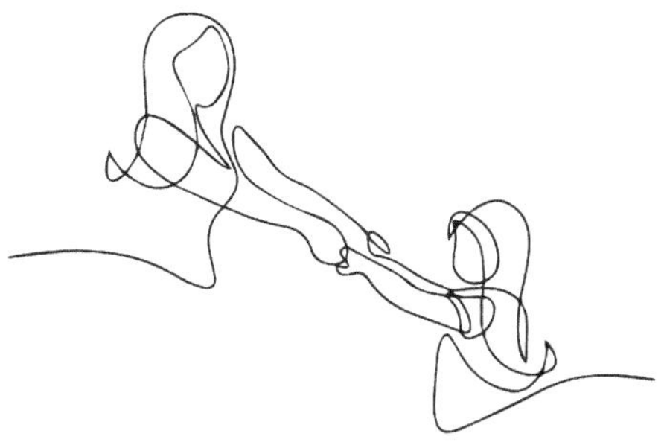

Every day as the clouds bled with hope,
My heart tenderly played jump rope,
Though my only challenge was crossing that
road,
But I was all of five, and had Maa's hand to
hold.

Life then was a treasure trove of confusion,
But Maa, you had an answer to every
question,
The more I aged, the more I learnt,
You were a superwoman, in a human cloak.

We grew together, even though apart,
But we knew we had each other's heart,
We laughed, we fought, in our uncanny bond,
You and I were - love, hate, and everything
beyond.

I've always been the one to explore,
Off on my own, to see what's in store,
But no matter where I went, or how much I
had grown,
I knew I'd have you waiting for me back
home.

Today, you're on your journey; far-far away,
But I still feel your presence every day,
I carry you with me, in all that I do,
For I am, oh, but a part of you.

Weight of Loss

I remember the stillness of that morning,
When you were wrapped in deep sleep,
I kissed you, whispering "I love you"
And counted promises I couldn't keep.

If only I had more time with you, I thought,
Or if I had realized that your life was short,
I'd break open to love you more,
And lull you, as we rowed to the shore.

Goodbyes were often said before,
But that morning shook my very core,
I know, you too had promises to keep,
And miles to go, before you sleep.

Each day in a world without you,
Is a battle effectively turning my soul blue,
And the longing of "what could be,"
Saddles my heart in all degree.

Sitting tight all day with your thoughts,
Is keeping me abreast of all my knots,
Hoping that grief will soon take a pause,
Because, oh, how heavy is this weight of loss.

Hope and Hurt

I'll tell you a tale of Hope and Hurt,
Where one was gaiety, and the other was curt.

They lived together in a half-knit home,
With their pasts intertwined in monochrome.

In the quiet corners of their shared abode,
The sounds of prayers and tears echoed.

Where hope rose to seize the day,
Hurt shone brightly in the night's grey.

Some days, they knocked each other down,
Leaving each other numb to fix their crown.

They questioned why they were even bound,
Oh, how their wounds were blue and
profound.

But they couldn't escape their rugged fate,
They knew together they must gracefully
navigate,

For the world danced to their ballet,
Without them, existence would crumble
away.

Lost and Found

Soaked in worldly literature,
Did you miss out on the bigger picture?
The colors in it were never tangible,
The words in it were always intelligible.

You swirled around in delusion,
Throwing your heart into immense confusion,
You nudged away your feelings,
Moved on, before completely healing.

Oh, they never taught you to be truly alive
To do only what pushes you to survive,
You achieved it all, in the end,
But only you could never be your own friend.

Now, in the stillness of your mind,
Seek the truths you left behind,
Embrace the feelings you once denied,
And find the peace you've long defied.

Grief

The world's a different color today,
Rosy tints are off and skies are grey,
This unbidden change has led me astray,
Down a corridor, showing me a new way.

The shades of my kin now appear deeper,
Giving me clarity of an avid reader,
The ones with love are emerging in need,
And hypocrites are gradually freed.

Oh, these new frames of truth confuse me,
Challenging everything I have ever seen,
What I once believed, in reality, wasn't,
Revealing gaps that were ever-present.

Marvel at the lesson the universe bestowed,
Each piece of the puzzle left questions untold,
Soon I reached the corridor's end in disbelief,
Realising all along my journey was Grief.

Letting Go

My heart's a home for a bundle,
But my mind's adjusting every muscle,
To greet those soaked in love's embrace,
And bear those cloaked in deceit's trace.

So my mind's stuck, trying to piece together,
'Why do I cling to voices that don't even
matter?'
I exhaust myself with forced courtesy,
Leaving my heart to endure days of misery.

The more I age, the more I see,
We must make room for self-love to be,
For what takes space isn't what I need,
But a burden of another's opinions, that must
be freed.

So I must bask in my unfiltered truth,
Embrace my life's reality, with the vigour of
youth,
And feel my heart and mind breathe in a
peaceful flow,
As I master the art of 'Letting Go'.

Demons

I wish we had met before we were broken,
Before our wretched scars had spoken,

I wish we met at a time when love awoke,
In a time when our hearts were far from
cloaked,

I wish it weren't so grueling to sail together,
But I love how we stuck tight through every
weather,

I know our love is under the spell of our
pasts,
But don't you wonder, what made our love
last?

How, yet again, everything falls into a perfect
grid,
Because my love, our demons found each
other way before our hearts did.

Versions of Me

Raised as a bird with periodic flaws,
Self-doubt was but my earned cause,
The more I flap, the more I see,
Others soar far more swiftly than me.

I flap harder, striving to shine,
In self-battle, I lose my sight,
Fixated solely on the finish line,
No room for love, no moment of delight.

You came along showing me love,
But I knew not who I truly was.
You love me today, but is that enough?
There are many versions of me, hidden in the rough.

The one I was, as a little girl,
Happy and bright like a polished pearl,
I loved myself then, that's all I recall,
I can never be her again, but will you love her
after all?

The one I was, when my heart broke,
Lonely and meek, buried in smoke,
I've recovered from that, but you might see her
again,
Will you love her too, in this loving bargain?

The one I wasn't, but always try,
The smartest of all, with the best wings to fly,
I long for holding onto her, once in a while,
Will you too, without a trial?

The one I couldn't be, for no fault of mine,
But I notice how the others got it so fine,
Some days I reek of envy and all that negativity,
Will you love her too? With all your ability?

Some days I'm not the version you adore,
But one - I'm still searching for,
So will you join me as I flap to the finish line,
And turn this journey into a fine glass of wine?

Perfect Love

The idea of love will addle your wit,
Because mind-over-matter will never commit,

And the thirst to err on the right side will
retire,
Leaving the kindred spirits much to desire.

Unrequited or mutual, never mind the type,
Expectation in love is but a burning pipe.

Smoke it or not, it'll turn to ash,
Wheeling heartbreak in a tiny flash.

Let's uncage love from the oversold 'perfect',
Caress its flaws as it confidingly strips naked,

And amidst those cracks when you find your
heart,
You can then hope to fiercely love, even the
broken parts.

A Happier Shore

Heartbreak to each is absurdly different,
Emotions indeed, are strange instruments,
Some swiftly rewind to a familiar groove,
Finding a response their inner child would
approve.

Hey! There's no better way to sail these waves,
But to journey where your younger self
braves,
And acknowledge them for how well they've
done,
Oh, their strength and spirit were never
undone.

It wasn't their fault when they weren't
understood,
Nor was it their place to be devalued,
Remind them of their growth through the
years,
And how you embrace yourself today, in all
your colours.

Honour them by standing firm in their own
strength,
Ensuring you keep self-doubt at arm's length,
Yes, you will sometimes fail to treat yourself
well,
But you'll gather strength and support from
your tribe's swell.

So take that leap into self-love's aisle,
And go on a date with your inner child,
Comfort them for the pain they've endured,
And lead them by hand-in-hand to a happier
shore.

Stride for Stride

The mountains call me like a folded mystery,
I leap to answer under the stars fearlessly,
My heart thumps fire at every sight,
Was this my home in another life?

On a silent night, a lost soul found me,
Shadowing close, on four paws, free,
As I watch her slip into a peaceful slumber,
Has she returned to me from a past life? I
wonder.

Soul tripping led me to an old abode,
With doors overwhelmed and windows
widowed,
And books with words that cut me deep
inside,
Echoing dreams from lives I lived and died.

Are we all drawn to the same old quest,
Seeking answers we can't possess?
Are we soldiers reborn to find our tribe?
Fighting the same wars, stride for stride?

Her Worth

Chirping birds and echoes of prayers,
Jolt her from her dreams in layers;
She swiftly stands awake, greeting the dawn,
Meeting expectations, of those long gone.

She carries the legacy of her late mother,
Or is it a burden cloaked in a fancy cover?
She's often told to keep it together,
And wear a smile, come any weather.

The day descends into a tiresome night,
She battles on, alone in her plight,
Rousing herself to work under pressure,
She wipes her tears as a silent measure.

The poetic moon and the chilly cold,
Lull her to sleep in a new day's hope,
May she soon find the strength to see
Her own worth, her own decree.

Healing

Healing takes a lot more than just time,
It takes your wit to ride the aching storm in
its prime,
Setting your heart aflame, to light every dark
day,
And then find hope, as the sky fades into a
familiar grey.

It takes your soul to keep a silent affair with
pain,
Letting your glass jaw take all the strain,
While your heart knits its brow to ease the
sore,
And your mind works to build an escape
door.

Healing takes more than just fidelity,
It takes you to caress each stitch breathlessly,
Invigorating your soul to cherish every scar,
And romancing every win within a whisker.

It takes you to fight and lead with your chin,
When the dark cloud once again breaks in,
It takes you to shoulder the truth that
restoring is uncertain,
And that feeling numb might be the
unsettling bargain.

Star Crossed Lovers

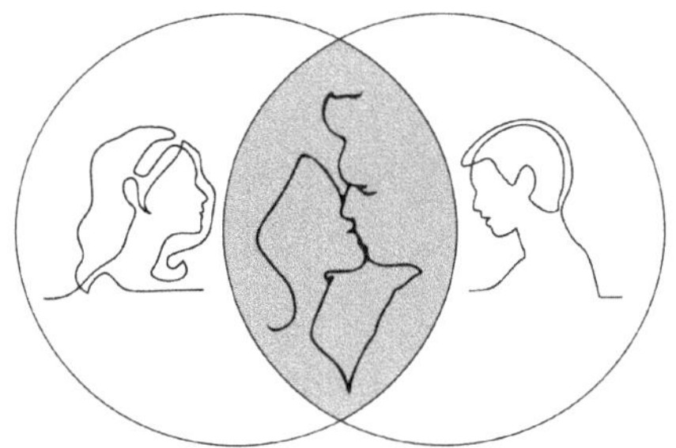

The letter of the word 'love' fall so steep,
Like pearls from my pen,
And begin to beat on the blank sheet,
Like my nervous heart in a dark den.

Each letter expressed a sweet pain,
And that reminded me of us once again,
Next to each other, it emitted a magical vibe,
Sometimes secretly pronounced as 'life'.

Every episode of our hurtful separation,
Drove me miles closer to desperation,
But I kept you warm in my heart,
For I knew, we could never be apart.

Our names are now taken together,
In stories that do not have a forever,
And all our trials are now done,
We are destined to never live as one.

But some stories are meant to shine through
their scars,
Like how you and I have, on the walls of our
hearts,
And ages after we're buried under layers,
We will unite again as Star Crossed Lovers.

Forever

The dawn of youth brings you a lover's glow,
And you share a first kiss as soft winds blow,
Do you remember the magic of your first love?
When your heart was a butterfly, soaring above.

You whispered and laughed in dreams together,
But your hands trembled when you embraced
each other,
You moved mountains together to be
hand-in-hand,
And you'd already know the world wouldn't
understand.

Oh, how simple life felt during that time,
No race to run, no battles to fight,
Only love could fill you, pure and bright,
And guide you through it all, day and night.

But as you grew, you knew love was tricky,
There was more to it than being just lucky,
It demanded patience, respect and care,
And brought moments of joy with times of
despair.

You'd have to choose, every day,
To break open your heart and love, in every
way,
Because love requires two pairs of steady hands,
To navigate life through shifting sands.

Mature love meant understanding,
The language your partner found enchanting,
Are you still searching for that first-love spark?
Don't. Because this one is fire, even in the dark!

The spark will fade, but love will endure,
Built on the journey, of ache and cure,
The first is cherished, yet may not sustain,
But a lasting love will forever remain.

Power of Now

Time sometimes has a knack for staying still,
Really! In its own way, but only at our will.

We could burn in the flames of our past,
Or float in its poetic moments till the very
last.

Or we could weave a better today,
Without dwelling on how tomorrow might
stray.

Let yesterday gracefully grow numb,
Because tomorrow may not even come.

So, wrap your heart in 'today' and bow,
To the everlasting power of 'Now'.

Perfect Artist

The only thing fun about falling apart,
Is the possibility to rebuild like a work of art,

Take a moment, though, to admire each piece,
And remember, there is still 'you' in every
crease.

Then bravely piece up into a new mould,
Soaked in hope, ready to take on the world.

But remember, there will be yet another rain,
And you will rebuild yourself, all over again.

So indulge in this journey to create 'you',
And I promise, each time you'll be a fresh
brew,

But remember to let go of the pieces that
parted,
For only then can you become the perfect
artist.

Home

There's a scar that takes us home,
Through valleys of pain where as children
we'd roam,
And meadows of hope painted in distant
chrome,
Where even time couldn't heal what was
perfectly sewn.

The comfort of home came at a hefty price,
One we paid over and over, never thinking
twice,
Its walls stood tall, masking a peaceful facade,
While the chaos inside broke our innocent
hearts.

What is love? What is hate?
We were buried under the weight,
Yet we clung to hope that the pain would
fade,
Never imagining our wounds would deepen
and cascade.

We escaped the grip of all that was toxic,
Yet, we felt trapped, our burdens were
chronic,
We fought, we struggled, we pushed our way
through,
But oh, home isn't always a place you can
return to.

Small Wins

'Tringgg Tringgg' rang my new alarm,
I stretched to hit snooze with a large yawn,
But I vowed to rise like a diligent lark,
So I reluctantly rolled out of bed in the
pre-dawn dark.

Graduating into the day, I met a fancy jerk,
Who's stubborn attitude was like the Devil's
work,
But I chose to be the one my dog thinks I am,
And managed my anger with a calm and
steady hand.

On my way to work came a fluffy stray,
His eyes were bright, had a smile to slay,
He cheered me up with his wagging tail,
Unlike the history of my emotional fail.

Small challenges try to weigh me down,
But I religiously resist without a frown,
With determination as my faithful guide,
I embrace my small wins with quiet pride.

Rediscover Hope

Oh, we've all been braving a storm,
One that tries us, rendering us reborn.

Oh, we're all resisting the grim failure,
One that makes us a fatigued sailor.

Oh, we're all buried in deep grief,
Mourning an absence, or just what we
couldn't be.

Oh, we've all led ourselves to war,
Combatting over what was absolutely bizarre.

Oh, we've all paid the price of love and hate,
One that sketched the details of our fate.

Oh, we've all indulged in the comforts of the
dark,
And when we didn't find the light - a fire
alone we'd spark.

Oh, we've all trodden the path of misery,
And found each other on this very journey.

Oh, we've all been lost a while, wandering to
cope,
Can we weave our stories together, to
rediscover hope?

Insanity

It roped them in,
They swore their heart knew this was a sin,

It clouded their sight,
They swore they ducked enough for all the
light.

It appeared at the spark of their smoke,
And patiently waited for them to become a
beautiful joke,

But there was contentment in its presence,

The type that made them forget their daily
lessons.

They couldn't sketch if it was right or wrong,
Or whether it made them weak or strong,

But they knew the darkness was their space
now,
With each step, it got darker and how.

And when they decided, "I'll make it mine"
They could only hear the chords, wind and
the chime,

For them, it was now mundanity,
But for everyone after today, it will be
insanity.

Thirty

Swirling my tiniest finger around your tallest
one,
I thought, after all life's battles, you're the
prize I've won.

Looking at your eyes so small and your
laughter so hearty,
I promised to be the best father; so what if
I'm just thirty?

Days filled with feeding, parenting, laughter,
and tears,
Watching you grow through the weeks,
months, and years.

In my invisible calendar, I noted each little
thing,
For making you smile was my daily offering.

And now you're on your own, and very much
in love,
With someone who holds your hand like a
newborn dove,

What is it that I can, but you can't see?
He can't look after you - he's just thirty!

Kindness

Kindness today is a note of suspicion,
To what do I owe this noble expression?
A favour you need, or a debt you repay,
Or a hidden agenda, that's underplayed?

Oh, I raised my vulnerable self this decade,
With no guard held, no heed paid,
So pardon me and my relentless confusion,
Trust right now is but a broken illusion.

How rarely was my kindness returned,
When it was, I believed it wasn't earned,
As I sailed away baffled in unrest,
There were waves of bitterness in my chest.

I learn now, I only witnessed the truth,
After choosing sweet delusions in my youth,
So, I swim to escape and break away,
But I find your gentle hand caving my way.

Yet caution whispers softly in my ear,
Your kindness shouldn't lead to regret, I fear,
But I accept your gesture, guard held high,
And I watch you gracefully love me, as I sigh.

Figment of my Imagination

I press my toes as I lean forward against the
glass,
Breathing warmth on the frosty window,
waiting for you to pass.

Hoping to wave at you, as you run towards
me,
But you disappear and there is nothing that I
can see.

I wipe the glass with my wrinkled hand,
So I can see you clearly, playing at the other
end.

Nothing has changed, everything is the same,
Come home soon, we'll play your favourite
game.

Your timely absence owes me an explanation,
Because everyone thinks, you are my mind's
creation.

Every night my arms are your haven,
Please, oh, please tell them,
You are not a figment of my imagination.

One day, One last time

One day, it might all end,
The pain you've endured with chaos in a
blend,
The darkest hours will slowly fade away,
So learn what you can from it today.

One day might be the last for that thought,
On an ordinary day, you'll finally have what
you've sought.
So feel the thought in it's acute charm,
For then you have wisdom and growth in
your palm.

One day might be the last time you hold
something dear,
Something you will long after wish was near.
So hold it now, like you never again will,
And savour it to its depth in loving thrill.

One day might be the final time you kiss,
A breezy moment that you might quietly
miss.
So love fiercely today, while time allows,
And cherish the now, not just the vows.

One day might be the last you can taste,
A favorite meal, with no moment to waste.
So relish the flavors, let them remain,
For the simplest joys are never in vain.

One day might mark the final embrace,
You'll have a hand to hold and a familiar face.
So take life in, don't let it slip,
For its core-memories are found in its grip.

Another Goodbye

It's been so long,
That I've repeatedly sung the same song,
Bringing an abundance of head-splitting pain,
That grows harder each day to explain.

The red on my nails mirrors the red on my
face;
I've practiced counting to find my calm place.
Because all of it, every bit, was you - my
anger,
An energy that only makes me stronger, yet
stranger.

Go back to wherever you came;
This space is for my people - find some shame.
Your power in my veins turns me into a beast,
While the composed me becomes your feast.

But this time, I'll fight you with grace,
So when you return, you'll come at a slower
pace,
And allow me to handle you like an ace,
So we might unite for a better cause, in
another place.

For now, I can look myself in the eye,
And feel good letting the negatives slide by,
Taking a step forward, watching my will
multiply,
Here's to bidding my anger another goodbye.

Freedom

I've told her more often than not,
'You're so lucky for the freedom you've got!'
Because freedom is sweet, that's all I could
see,
But she paid a price that scraped her knee.

She's gone to war for this fragile grace,
Shed countless tears with a hidden face,
Given up more than she could ever own,
Felt hollowed out, when cast alone.

But consumed and hurt, I watched her rise,
With strength reborn under open skies,
For every wound and scar she bore,
Was proof of courage and a powerful core.

And in her rise, she lights the way,
For others seeking freedom, every day,
The price of freedom may be heavy,
But what you gain is oh, so worthy!

Forgive

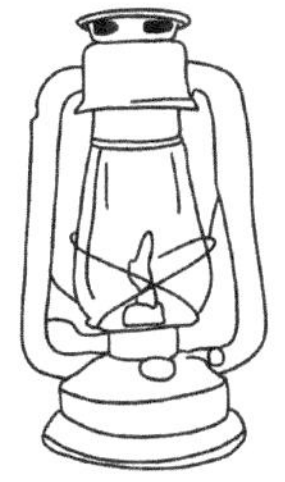

Some losses carve us deeper,
Lingering like a stubborn fever.
What's taken feels inevitable,
Yet not every act is punishable.

Some wounds arise from another's pain,
A cycle of hurt where none can gain.
They show us scars from where they came,
Trapped in a shadow, lost to blame.

Yet we grow despite what we must bear,
With healing found in broken air.
In time, each bruise may not fade- but will pass,
Leaving strength where sorrow was cast.

From all that hurt, wisdom bloomed,
Though they say that the one who hurt is
forever doomed.
I learn each day to keep the pain, release the
bitter,
And slowly forgive, for my vigour.

The Father

Maybe it isn't about love,
Or the life you gave me, which I'm so proud
of,
It isn't even about the hurt,
Though that's the reason for feelings to assert.

It's really about my freedom,
A word you see as a shadow, almost a demon.
And if I dare to reach for it, come what may,
You stand there, judging, as if I've strayed.

So may I indulge, from a little to a lot,
To live freely, till, of course, I get caught.
Yet you must know, it's been a heavy fight,
To feel so deeply and conceal it from sight.

So may I write my story, bold and bare,
Hoping that courage outshines despair.
And while I do, might I find a friend,
In a loving father, who lets my tale begin, not
end.

Becoming Us

It took only a moment to fall in love with
you,
But to truly rise in it, - let me take my time.

I'm learning to make peace with my
emptiness,
And to embrace yours, let me take my time.

My doubts hold me close, they've kept me
safe,
But to let your light in, please let me take my
time.

With each passing day, I sink deeper into this
love,
Yet to face the pain that may come, let me
take my time.

Layers of walls guard my soul, built strong
and high,
But to let them fall, please let me take my
time.

I've changed more than you know, grown in
so many ways,
But to fit the outline of your dreams, let me
take my time.

Home in You

In you, I find the warmth of my perfectly
brewed tea,
The comfort of my well-worn, favourite tee.

In you, there's the embrace of my old pillow,
And the echo of my childhood laughter,
mellow.

You are the sun breaking through on a cold,
grey day,
The sense of safety when doors close and
shadows stay.

You're the scent of a book that feels like a friend,
The stroke of my brush, where colours softly blend.

Stay, for I have yet to weave you into my lines,
Stay, for I've yet to make you a verse that shines.

Stay, for I am yet to draw you nearer to love,
Stay, for I am yet to be the home you dream of.

The Story We Live

The story you tell yourself matters the most,
It fuels your courage like a risen toast.

Be kind to yourself and gently bloom,
Sabotage your thoughts, and you welcome
gloom.

The choice is yours to tell what you must,
Lo and behold, it is you, whom you must
trust.

Truth or illusion, the narrative is yours,
The life you live begins at this very source.

Show yourself care, and let love unfold,
Treat your heart like a treasure trove of gold.

For the tale you spin will guide your way,
Manifesting sunshine in the shadowed gray.

Trust your instincts, hear your soul's plea,
Drop the shame and set your pride free.

Each word you choose rewrites your light,
So stay close to your truth and keep it in
sight.

Tiny Kicks, Big Dreams

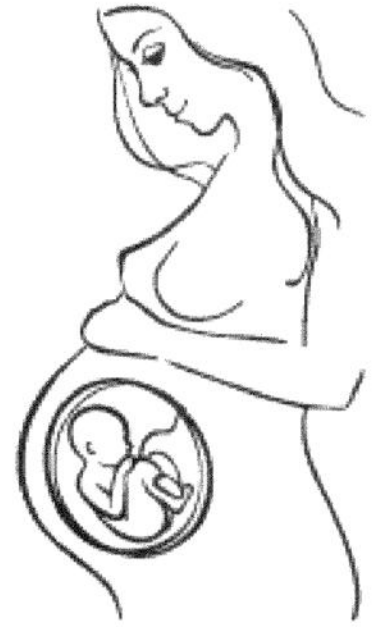

Taking the last sip of my sugarless morning
tea,
I smile, knowing you're yearning for
something sweet.

I'm thrilled to feel your first little kick,
A sign that you're with me, whenever you
pick.

It feels just right, like my own private bubble,
I wait in patience, knowing joy will soon
double.

I keep you safe inside, a secret so deep,
Lying on my back, cradling you in peaceful
sleep.

No matter how heavy my body may grow,
The thought of bringing you to life makes my
heart glow.

I stay busy, building you and your dream
space,
Just like my mother did, with love and grace.

Counting the months, one-two-three...-eight,
Soon you'll be here, and my world will feel
complete.

Destiny's Bet

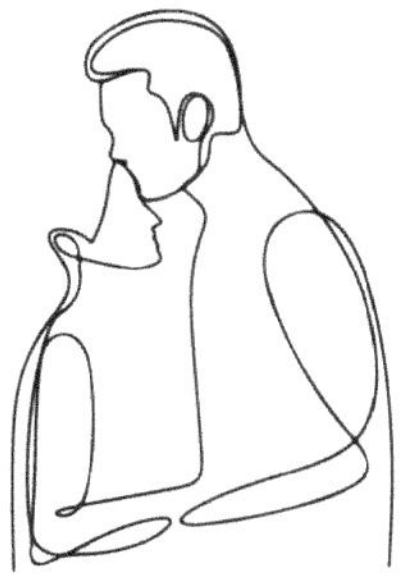

What if I told you,
I played a trick to make you mine,
Fought against my world and time,
Rehearsed my words, perfected every line.

What if I told you,
We never would have met,
Had I not spun my net,
And made my heart win this bet.

What if I told you,
I dreamed of you day and night,
To never let you slip from sight,
And fill our lives with endless light.

What if I told you,
All my promises may change,
But my heart will always be within range,
As destiny unfolds, we'll find our way
Together, come what may.

Feelings

Some standing numb behind the walls - torn
apart,
Some with a heart of its own, like a work of
art,
And some breathing perfectly fine, with hope
to restart,
But all of them - dead or alive - still exist in
my heart.

Even after all these complicated feelings,
I'm told I lack the intimacy that's healing,
Maybe they're somewhere amid their
mending,
Or are they dead, for good or bad, engraved
in my heart's ending?

All of this makes me float in waves of
emotion,
Challenging my intellect, stirring a stormy
ocean.
How do I calm them and avoid this explosion,
Protecting my world from a dangerous
commotion?

I guess even my whole life isn't enough,
To learn how to deal with them when they
show up.
Maybe it's not so bad to be overwhelmed,
Because in the end, it's only me who'll steady
my helm.

But even as I struggle to find my way,
I've learned to rise from the ashes of dismay.
So I sharpened my pencil, let my thoughts
take flight,
And in this chaos, I found my light.

Scarred

As I lay with my guitar,
Outstaring a lonely star,
Playing the deepest chords,
I drop all my guards.

And then let love dance into my arms,
Caressing me with all its charm.
Ah, it's amazing how it feels on my skin,
When this familiar feeling breaks in.

But I knew I'd have to let it go,
For I was but a painted doe,
Stripped of all, heading home,
Yet my star followed me into the storm.

It promised to calm the chaos inside,
Each time giving me a fresh guide,
To a peace that could never truly be,
But isn't that a poet's misery?

But oh, let me gather myself again,
Shake off every grain of pain,
And once again be rendered off-guard,
Ready to embrace all that's scarred.

Perfect Brew

I remember the first time I met you,
A splash of colour, almost unreal,
"Was it from you?" I wondered,
Cupid's arrow suddenly thundered.

My world wore a filter of your thoughts,
Like a poet's dream of endless applause,
Everything else took a gentle pause,
For the universe had drawn a destined cause.

And the strangest feeling came true,
I was a teenage girl again, from high school,
If asked, "What are you smiling about?"
I'd say "nothing," yet you'd fill my thoughts.

"Could I just hold your hand?" you asked,
Instead, you pulled me in and kissed me at
last.
That moment should've frozen in time,
Or perhaps been a dreamy, endless rhyme.

"Is this really meant to be?" I thought,
What makes me shudder, with feelings I've
fought?
Do these questions even have answers,
Or has my heart already become your graceful
dancer?

Ahh, so many feelings... they overwhelm me,
Especially the ones for you, that set me free.
The warmth of your heart is my kind of
perfect brew,
Tell me, how could I have not fallen for you?

Draw me Near

Most days I'd rather stay aloof,
Declutter thoughts of you, as they disapprove,
Then lay you in my worn-out puzzle,
And love you hard with every muscle.

Most days I'd rather live in my mind,
Where I could blur every margin behind,
Where love didn't need to conceal and hide,
Where it wouldn't matter if I was or wasn't
your bride.

So let me stay close, draw me near,
In this love, I've nothing to fear.
For in you, I've found my home,
In your heart, I'm never alone.

Bound by Love

I still remember that quiet evening,
When your touch was so gentle, like the softest
feeling.
I still remember waking up next to you,
In a space unknown, yet everything felt true.

I still remember how you'd guide me through
the day,
With your love, lighting the way.
Your hands would gently pull me from the dark,
Your love was my constant, like an eternal
spark.

I still remember how you'd protect me from
harm,
With your love and strength, I felt so warm.

We'd talk about dreams we wanted to share,
Knowing together, we'd make them real with
care.

I still remember the warmth in your voice,
Telling me I was your choice.
To walk beside you, to be your bride,
In your love, I'd forever abide.

I still remember how you began to see me,
Not just as a lover, but as someone truly free.
I became the one you'd trust with your heart,
And in that moment, we'd never be apart.

I still remember when you held my hand tight,
Together we'd face the darkest night.
My heart swelled with a love so pure,
In your embrace, I was always sure.

I still remember all the things we left behind,
Every fear, every doubt, in the back of my mind.
Because with you, I found what was true,
My heart was yours, and yours was mine too.

You

I'm tired of hitting backspace,
On every word that fails to trace,
The depth of you, so vast, so true,
And here I am, with a blank sheet, and you.

My tea remains, not yet turned cold,
And here I sit, in this same old hold,
The same feelings, the same waiting game,
For you, who still feels like a burning flame.

I remember walking through your narrow
door,
To find you sitting, just as I swore,

Your sparkling eyes, like satin bright,
Wrapped around me, pulling me into the
light.

In those five seconds, I wished for time to
freeze,
To explain how my heart would never cease,
Rising in love with you, a million times,
With every second, every rhyme.

I wanted to touch your darkest side,
And kiss your brightest, with nothing to hide.
To make you my escape, my lifetime's plea,
For you to be all, and forever mine to be.

What we leave behind

Years of hustle, striving high,
Chasing dreams I couldn't deny.
A great life promised if I stayed on track,
But would I be proud when I look back?

It's in the journey that I came to see,
Life's meaning was never a degree.
What truly counted, what left its mark,
Were the times I chased an open spark.

Those times I took a step off-track,
Carried my life in a rusty backpack,
Lived to crack open core memories,
Now I see them as small victories.

When I look back, I remember my dogs,
Their wagging tails like joyful applause.
I remember painting as a little girl,
With life-sized canvases, dreams unfurled.

I remember how fiercely I loved,
How many fears I unpacked and ungloved,
How strong I stood in the test of time,
The paths I wandered, how they made me
shine.

But I don't recall the teams I led,
Or the sums of money that filled my head.
What stays instead, clear as an echo,
Are the lives I touched in moments mellow.

How silly are we in life, I think,
Chasing fleeting things gone in a blink.
Not titles or wealth, nor grand designs,
Just the love and moments we leave behind.

Breath by Breath

The universe stands as mighty proof,
With stars above, my sacred roof.
I long for you, your tender touch,
To color my heart's canvas with your brush.

But I bow gracefully to the notes of nature,
Knowing in one world, we'll be written
together,
Knit closely, to be in love, to share a life,
And stand before the world as man and wife.

Hands on our hearts, we cherish and yearn,
Trusting that love is what we'll earn.
Patiently we wait, for the day to arrive,
When side by side, we'll truly come alive.

Until then, in dreams, we find our way,
Through whispered words, we silently pray,
Two souls apart, yet aligned in depth,
Guided by love, breath by breath

Wisdom in the Puzzle

Our mind is a daunting puzzle,
The pretty and ugly put in a bundle.
The end game we're yet to choose,
Pick wisely, or risk your mind to lose.

Each puzzle piece is a thought you hold,
Connect it with another, is strength so bold.
Leave it behind, is a thought you let go,
Make sure you release only those - that dim
your glow.

Be mindful of what you pay heed to,
Because in your life, that stays with you.
Choose for yourself only love and care,
What you will suffer for, what will you dare?

What would you do, how best would you live?
Who must you let go, who must you forgive?
How would you fiercely love your tribe?
Would you be proud of this life, when you
die?

Your thoughts shape each twist, each turn,
Yet mistakes are lessons, not cause for
concern.
Acknowledge them along the way, no matter
big or small,
For wisdom grows by gently discerning them
all.

The Gift of Paws

A few years back, our lives forever changed,
When each one of you joined us, unplanned
and unarranged.
Since then, between your howls, gentle paws,
and yearning eyes,
Our world has grown in ways we never
realized.

With you, we learn what it means to love,
A trust so deep, soft as a dove.
You teach us patience, to take it slow,
To savor each day, to let moments flow.

Your wagging tails your playful ways,
Turn ordinary hours into golden days.
Of all life's gifts, the laughter, the cheers,
Each one of you is what we hold most dear.

To be your family, to be by your side,
Fills us with a joy we can never hide.
In your boundless love, we've found a home
With you, our hearts will never be alone.

Shells of her Heart

My Mum was an artist, with a heart full of
grace,
She was in awe of sea shells, scanning each
trace.

Every design to her was a spark of inspiration,
Nature was her teacher, with endless creation.

She'd wander the beaches, soaked in sunshine,
Picking the most beautiful shells to build her
design.

With delicate hands, she'd craft them into art,
A masterpiece formed from her soul and her
heart.

And today, in the shells, I found a way,
To feel close to you in my own quiet way.

A tribute to your love, your art, your shine,
I hope, Mumma, this one feels just fine.

The Tough

They said, be 'Tough', to handle 'Tough',
Or just let it run you over, soon enough.

So I put up a fair fight, like the winner's
choice,
And before I knew it, I found my lost voice.

But I missed the details in the bargain,
Which cost me leftovers, leaving me starving.

While Tough is busy being quite Tough,
We patiently wait for each storm to grab us
by the scruff,

Dragging us through, as we hang in tight,
And then some of us choose a very different
flight.

Whispers of You

Even though you aren't here today,
I felt you closer in every way.

When I cooked and it turned out like your
dish,
In a quiet moment, I wished you'd taste it.

When I parted my hair in a certain style,
And saw you in the mirror for a while.

When I wore your favorite dress,
I heard your voice, soft and blessed.

When I watched a movie you loved,
I replayed the scenes you dearly adored.

You'll always be with me, warm and true,
Wrapped in my grief and my love for you.

Unseen

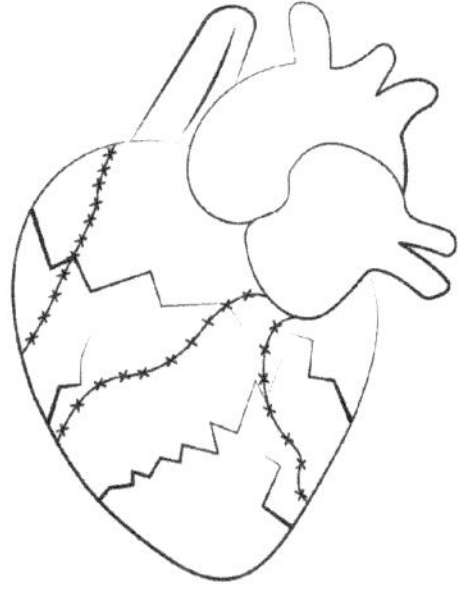

Oh!
There are bruises that you don't see,
and others bear,

Their world is burnt,
in a moment of despair.

So let's be grateful,
let's be kind,

Let's find that peace,
in the chaos of our mind.